Books by Patricia David

Hugs Inc.

This book serves as an informational tool for anyone, most notably children diagnosed with cancer.

Pat David provides terminology for all to understand with a humorous, uplifting twist to promote hope, understanding, guidance, and support (HUGS) as key factors in the healing process.

There's a Troll in a Bowl,

is designed to help the reader grasp a basic understanding of Energy Sound Healing.

The characters present the subject matter in a humorous manner with the purpose of involving readers of all ages.

Winnie's Victory

By

Patricia (Pat) David

Star Publishing
Myrtle Beach, South Carolina 29588
stareditors@gmail.com

Winnie's Victory
Copyright © 2014
Patricia David

All rights reserved.
This publication may not be reproduced, stored in
a retrieval system, or transmitted in any form, recording,
mechanical, electronic, or photocopy, without written
permission of the author.
The only exception is brief quotations used
in book reviews.

Comments.
Author email: gd0936@sccoast.net

Illustrations by OBD

ISBN: 978-1-941069-17-2

Star Publishing
Myrtle Beach, South Carolina 29588
stareditors@gmail.com

Dedication

This book is dedicated to all children diagnosed with cancer. You are inspirations, you are brave, and you are strong. Like Winnie, keep smiling as you weave your way through this journey of pediatric cancer. Your families are often scared and bewildered, but they are by your sides, holding your hands, loving you unconditionally.

I would like to thank all animal rescue shelters for providing hope and a new life for every abandoned, abused, hungry, and neglected member of the animal kingdom.

Additionally, I would like to acknowledge all Service Dog training centers. Our veterans are often challenged by health and psychosocial issues upon their return from deployments and these amazing, canines render life saving techniques with loyalty and love. Thank you to all of the trainers, volunteers and veterinarians who provide this service.

Lastly, I want to express my gratitude to all Veterans for your service to our Country. I have my freedom of self expression because of your sacrifices. For this I am eternally grateful.

I am challenging all who purchase this book to donate to local children's hospital pediatric cancer centers, animal rescue shelters or service dog training centers, but please do not forget our veterans. There are many local veteran service organizations who could use financial assistance.

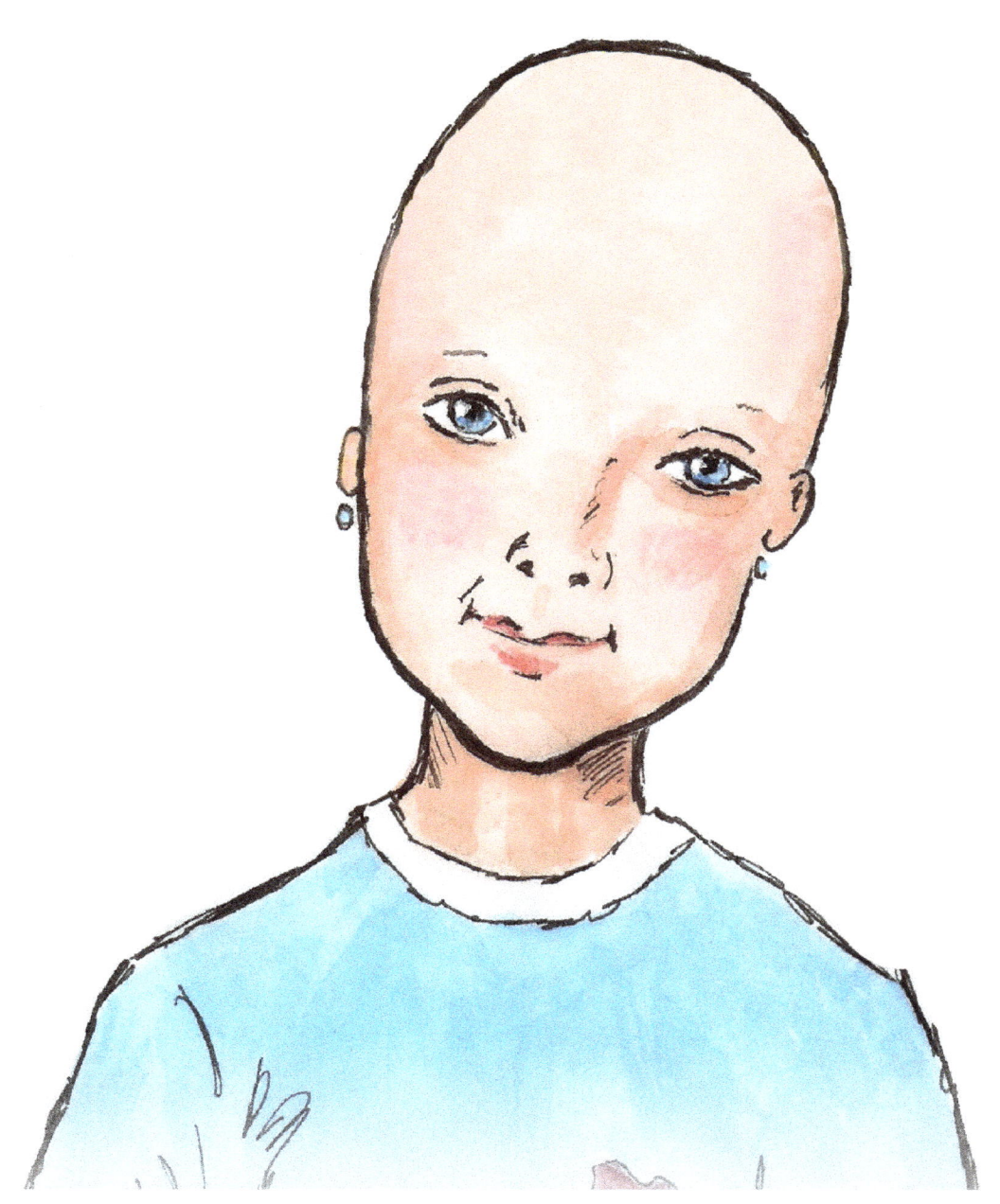

Chapter One

Hi there my name is Winnie. I am 10 years old. I live at the beach in South Carolina and have I got a story for you.

It's all about many kinds of heroes.
You know folks just like the ones in this book, because, they come from hometowns just like yours and do amazing things for others.

There's a magical, talking dog who writes and who is most definitely a hero too.

So let's get started.

A year ago I had cancer and was at the Children's Hospital.

About the same time, a Pit Bull pup was found on the side of the road hurt, hungry, and sick.

A kind man took her to an animal hospital where a veterinarian and his helpers gave her medicine and love, just like the doctors and nurses at the Children's Hospital did for me.

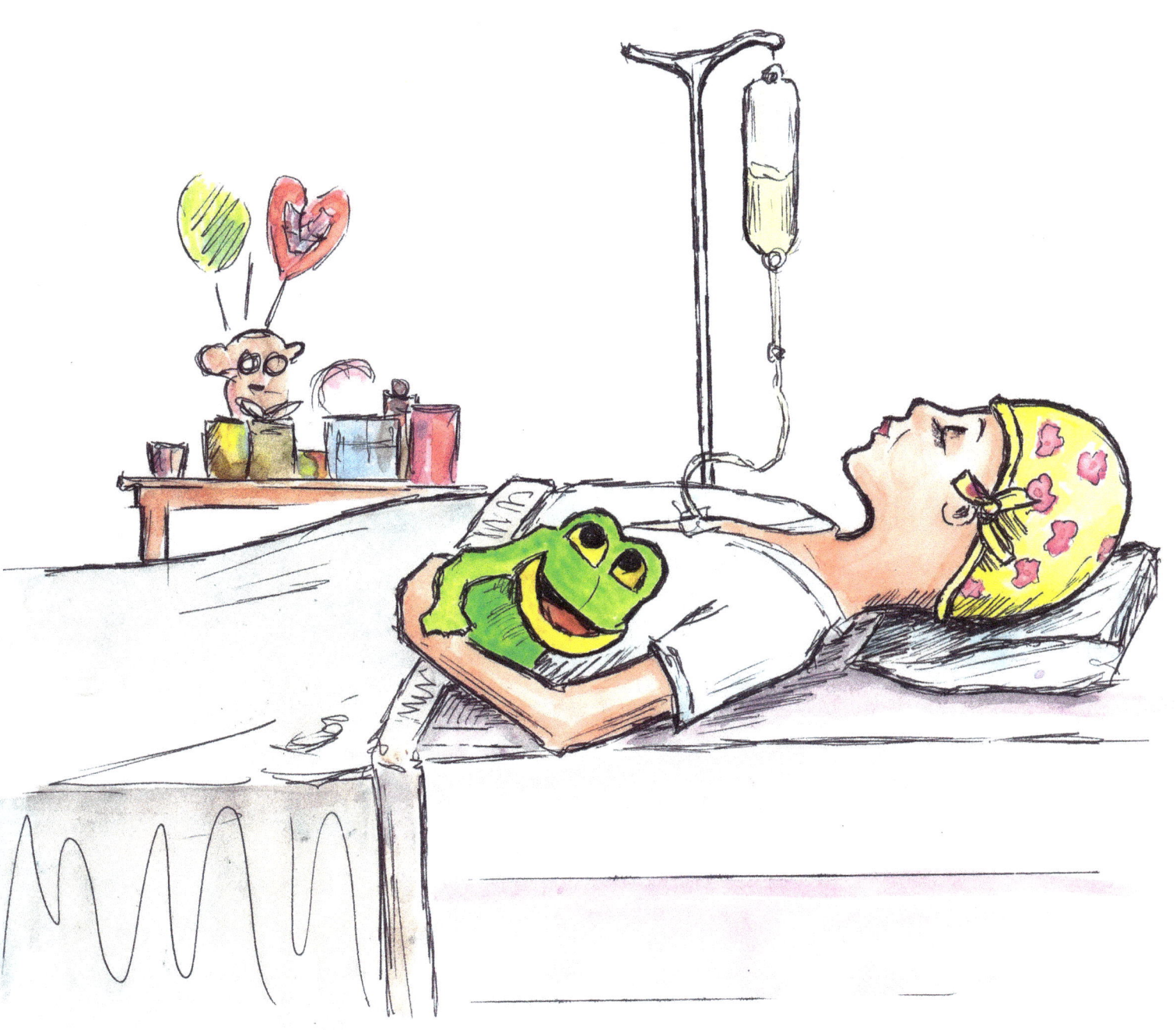

When that little pup got better, she was put in a shelter with all the other dogs
waiting to be adopted.

She smiled and wagged her tail but no one was interested because she was a Pit Bull.

People are sometimes afraid of Pit Bulls because some folks train them to be mean,

but, I know that
Pit Bulls are happy and give lots of love.*their

When my treatments were done, I wanted to do
something good for all the help I got
during my illness.

Guess what?

We went to that same animal shelter to rescue a dog.

I was so excited.

I came to the cage where the little Pit Bull was sleeping.
I thought she was the most, beautiful dog I had ever seen.

And you know what?

That dog jumped up wagging her tail staring right at me.

I couldn't stop myself and shouted,
"I want this one Mom, please?"

"We'll see Winnie, I'm just not sure," said Mom.

She knew that Pit Bulls have had bad things said about them and was a little worried.

A man came up to us and said he trains dogs to serve our country's veterans.

Veterans are those hometown heroes who fight in wars for freedom.

A lot of these men and women have disabilities. Some can't walk and are in wheel chairs, some can't hear, and some can't see. Some veterans have bad dreams because of things that happened in the war. This man was looking for another dog to rescue so that he could train it to be a service dog.

It's as if a light bulb went on inside my head.

I knew right away what I had to do.

I told the man,
"I am going to rescue this dog.
I'll be her foster mom and
you can train her for a very
special, veteran.

What do you think?

What's your name Mr.?"

My name is Jim and who are you young lady?"

"I'm Winnie and this is my mom. I'm just starting to get better from having cancer. Saving this dog will help her and I think she'll help me, too.

Look at her tail wag. She's the one for me."

Well, he liked my idea.

He asked if it would it be ok if he could train her for me and the veteran.

He reminded me, though, that it might be hard for me to let her go.

Mom couldn't wait either and said,
"It's a deal, Mr. Jim."

So what kind of commands are we going to have to know?"

"Oh, that's easy. All dogs have to do their doggie business so, they need to let you know when it's time to go outside.

They need to learn that they should not beg or jump on folks. They also need to know how to walk on a leash. You can train them to sit and stay, too."

Then he surprised me with, "Hey Winnie, we have to give her a name. What do you think about Dixie? After all, we live in the South."

With eyes as big as saucers I squealed, "I think we should name her Victory because she and her soon to be veteran owner have survived many battles; that's a true victory.

What do you think, Mr. Jim?"

"Victory it is. Now let's get her to the Veterinarian for a final check up. I'll give you a harness and vest, 'cause all service dogs wear them when they are working. Remind me to give you a bed and crate. Crates make dogs feel safe."

Chapter Two

It's been a few months since we brought Victory home and I think she's just perfect. Mr. Jim did a great job training her. Mom and I love walking her in our neighborhood. Heck we even take walks on the beach in the early morning. Is it ever funny watching her chase the waves. Oh how I remember the day a crab bit her right on her nose.
She yelled, "Help Winnie!"
That dog is magical.

The other day Mr. Jim stopped by with news that he has a Veteran who is having those bad dreams. Adults call them nightmares. "Here's how we train the service dog," he said,
"When the Veteran is having a nightmare the dog wakes them up and then cuddles with them to make them feel safe."

That's so cool, Mr. Jim but I'm feeling sad about giving her to anyone. I promise that I'll let her go but this is going to be hard for me."

"You know, Winnie, the veterans aren't just the heroes here. You fought the fight of your life. I think you are just as much a hero in a different way."

"I'm a kid who had cancer but there are many more kids in hospitals fighting this illness, and boy could they ever use a dog like Victory. Thanks to her I'm the happiest I've been in a long time."

Then I went to my room and cried.

Chapter Three

The next day we went to Mr. Jim's to meet Victory's new owner. I was really sad but reminded myself that I did this to help a veteran.

His name is Josh and he's kind of cute. He's very tall with a nice smile.

I noticed that Victory stared at him just like she did with me when I first saw her at the shelter.

I gave her a big goodbye hug.

I was so proud of myself, I didn't cry until Mom and
I got into the car.
Oh how I cried, all the way home, wondering if I'd
ever see Victory again. Then one Monday afternoon,
when I got home from school, there was a letter
waiting for me on the kitchen table,
it was from Victory!

Remember when I told you she was magical
and she could talk and write?

Here's what it said:

Dear Winnie,
I know how hard it was for you to let me go. Josh
is kind and a wonderful owner but I will always
remember you. Mr. Jim trained Josh and me together.
I wake him up when he's having nightmares and
we cuddle. He says that I make him feel safe again.

We even passed a big test we call a certification. You'd be so proud of me.

This will make you laugh. When I first went to Josh's home he had a really small bed. I don't know how many times I fell on the floor after we started to cuddle. Well, one night when I woke him from a nightmare, I jumped in bed, we both fell asleep then suddenly we both fell out of bed landing on the floor and all we could do was laugh. You should have seen me Winnie. I rolled on to my back and I can honestly say I couldn't stop laughing. The very next day Josh bought a bed big enough for both of us.

Josh is a hero Winnie. He says that he's just a guy like other soldiers who believe in freedom. He tells everybody that you made his life so much happier. Thank you for wanting to save me because he believes that I most certainly saved him. One more thing, you

are a brave girl who fought cancer then you rescued me; you are my hero.
Love and lots of doggie kisses,
Victory

P.S. Tell everyone this isn't the end. It's just the beginning of many stories. Now it's their turn to become a hero. Start by looking up service dogs for veterans on the internet and please volunteer or donate to their local Service Dog Training Center. Heck, we have centers right here in South Carolina and I know they're located all over the Country.

There are lots of lonely animals out there too, so think about helping out at an animal shelter or maybe even adopting a cat or dog. They sure do give lots of love. I'm a shelter graduate. Just a year ago I was lost, cold, hungry, and hurt until someone rescued me.

After a lot of happy tears I know that Mom and I made the right choice to rescue Victory. That letter is framed and sits on my bookcase. It makes me understand what it truly means to help.

So now I'm asking everyone to remember our Veterans. These men and women served our Country to give us the freedom we have today. Try to honor them by going to parades and celebrations. Remember to fly the flag on all the patriotic holidays and every time you see a soldier thank them for their service.

Thank You Veterans.

Chapter 4

I've decided to go back to the shelter to rescue another dog and Mr. Jim promises to work with me again. He's quite the hero, too, you know. This man trains dogs to save Veterans. Isn't that something?

My biggest surprise is that I'll be volunteering at the Children's Hospital Cancer Center. I am going to help kids who just found out they have cancer by telling my story. Keep an eye out for me 'cause this is just the beginning of a lot of adventures.

See y'all real soon!

Winnie's Victory Bibliography

Colin, Chris. "How Dogs Can Help Veterans Overcome PTSD." July, 2012. <http://www.smithsonianmag.com/science-nature/how-dogs-can-help-veterans-overcome-ptsd-137582968/.>

Collier Cool, Lisa. "A War Hero's Best Friend." Woman's Day. 2012. >http://womansday.com/life/pet-care/ptsd-dogs-for-veterans.>

Higgins, Jessie. "New Group that helps vets with PTSD debuts at parade/video." November 9, 2013. <http://www.courierpress.com/news/2013/nov/09/new-group-that-helps-vets-with-ptsd-debuts-at/?print=1.>

O'Reilly, Christie, CNN. "Service Dogs Help Veterans Heal (VID." November 11, 2013. <http://www.globalanimal.org/2013/11/11/service-dogs-help-veterans-heal-video/.>

PAALS Pack. "Palmetto Animal Assisted Life Services – Service Dogs, Assistance Dogs for

Soldiers with PTSD, Children with Autism, Mobility Challenged Individuals." February, 2012. >http://paals.org/w-pcontent/uploads/2012/02/paalspack.png>.

Paws Training Centers. "Service Dog Training." January 19, 2014 <http://pawstrainingcenters.com/dog-training/service>.

Service Dog Central. "Welcome to Service Dog Central." http://www.servicedogcentral.org/content/.

Vets Adopt Pets. "Service Dog Providers for Veterans." 2011. http://vetsadoptpets.org/vetsservicedogs.html.

Welker, Grant. "Groton woman trains dogs to help returning veterans through Chelmsford-based agency." July 7, 2013 < http://www.lowellsun.com>.

Working Like Dogs. "Service Dog Training Programs: Southeast." 2014. http://www.workinglikedogs.com/service-dog-resources/service-dog-training-programs-se/. >

www.ingramcontent.com/pod-product-compliance
Lightning Source LLC
Chambersburg PA
CBHW041433040426
42451CB00023B/3498